Native American Library

OJIBWE
History and Culture

Helen Dwyer and Sierra Adare

Consultant Robert J. Conley
Sequoyah Distinguished Professor at Western Carolina University

Gareth Stevens
Publishing

Please visit our website, www.garethstevens.com. For a free color catalog of all our high-quality books, call toll free 1-800-542-2595 or fax 1-877-542-2596.

Library of Congress Cataloging-in-Publication Data

Dwyer, Helen.
Ojibwe history and culture / Helen Dwyer and Sierra Adare.
   p. cm. — (Native American library)
Includes index.
ISBN 978-1-4339-7422-9 (pbk.)
ISBN 978-1-4339-7423-6 (6-pack)
ISBN 978-1-4339-7421-2 (library binding)
1. Ojibwa Indians—History. 2. Ojibwa Indians—Social life and customs. I. Birchfield, D. L., 1948- II. Title.
E99.C8D94 2012
977.004'97333—dc23

               2011045576

New edition published in 2013 by
Gareth Stevens Publishing
111 East 14th Street, Suite 349
New York, NY 10003

First edition published 2005 by Gareth Stevens Publishing

Copyright © 2013 Gareth Stevens Publishing

Produced by Discovery Books
Project editor: Helen Dwyer
Designer and page production: Sabine Beaupré
Photo researchers: Tom Humphrey and Helen Dwyer
Maps: Stefan Chabluk

Photo credits: Sierra Adare: p. 19 (bottom); Corbis: pp. 10, 13, 15, 19 (top), 21, 22, 26, 27, 32 (Ed Kashi), 33, 34; Getty Images: p. 35 (Bruce Bennett; bottom); Mille Lacs band (Minnesota): pp. 11, 16, 17, 23, 24, 25, 35 (top), 36, 37, 38; Peter Newark's American Pictures: p. 14; North Wind Picture Archives: p. 12; Shutterstock.com: pp. 5 (Jim Feliciano), 28 (IRC), 29 (Renaud Thomas); Sun Valley/Nativestock Photography: pp. 18, 20; Wikimedia: pp. 7 (Charles A. Zimmermann), 8, 31 (Hans-Jürgen Hübner), 39 (Donna Avalone/FEMA Photo Library).

Printed in the United States of America

CPSIA compliance information: Batch #CS12GS: For further information contact Gareth Stevens, New York, New York at 1-800-542-2595.

CONTENTS

Words that appear in the glossary are printed in **boldface** type the first time they appear in the text.

INTRODUCTION

The Ojibwes, or Chippewas, are a people of the Great Lakes region in both the United States and Canada. They are just one of the many groups of Native Americans who live today in North America. There are well over five hundred Native American tribes in the United States and more than six hundred in Canada. At least three million people in North America consider themselves to be Native Americans. But who are Native Americans, and how do the Ojibwes fit into the history of North America's native peoples?

Probable extent of dry land during the last ice age

CHUKCHI SEA

SIBERIA

Bering Strait

ALASKA

CANADA

BERING SEA

Anchorage

Siberia (Asia) and Alaska (North America) are today separated by an area of ocean named the Bering Strait. During the last ice age, the green area on this map was at times dry land. The Asian ancestors of the Ojibwes walked from one continent to the other.

THE FIRST IMMIGRANTS

Native Americans are people whose **ancestors** settled in North America thousands of years ago. These ancestors probably came from eastern parts of Asia. Their **migrations** probably occurred during cold periods called **ice ages**. At these times, sea levels were much lower than they are now. The area between northeastern Asia and Alaska was dry land, so it was possible to walk between the continents.

Scientists are not sure when these migrations took place, but it must have been more than twelve thousand years ago. Around that time, water levels rose and covered the land between Asia and the Americas.

By around ten thousand years ago, the climate had warmed and was similar to conditions today. The first peoples in North America moved around the continent in small groups, hunting wild animals and collecting a wide variety of plant foods. Gradually these groups spread out and lost contact with each other. They developed separate **cultures** and adopted lifestyles that suited their **environments.**

The Ojibwes believe they migrated from the East Coast, along the Saint Lawrence River to the Great Lakes and beyond.

The Cliff Palace at Mesa Verde, Colorado, is the most spectacular example of Native American culture that survives today. It consists of more than 150 rooms and pits built around A.D. 1200 from sandstone blocks.

SETTLING DOWN

Although many tribes continued to gather food and hunt or fish, some Native Americans began to live in settlements and grow crops. Their homes ranged from underground pit houses and huts of mud and thatch to dwellings in cliffs. By 3500 B.C., a plentiful supply of fish in the Pacific Ocean and in rivers had enabled people to settle in large coastal villages from Alaska to Washington State. In the deserts of Arizona, more than two thousand years later, farmers constructed hundreds of miles of **irrigation** canals to carry water to their crops.

The Ojibwe lifestyle changed with the seasons. They fished and grew crops in the summer, gathered wild foods in the fall, and hunted through the winter.

In the Ohio River valley between 700 B.C. and A.D. 500, people of the Adena and Hopewell cultures built clusters of large burial mounds, such as the Serpent Mound in Ohio, which survives today. In the Mississippi **floodplains**, the native peoples formed complex societies. They created mud and thatch temples on top of flat earth pyramids. Their largest town, Cahokia, in Illinois, contained more than one hundred mounds and may have been home to thirty thousand people.

CONTACT WITH EUROPEANS

Around A.D. 1500, European ships reached North America. The first explorers were the Spanish. Armed with guns and riding horses, they took over land and forced the Native Americans to work for them. The Spanish were followed by the British, Dutch, and French, who were looking for land to settle and for opportunities to trade. The Ojibwes came into contact with the French in 1622.

When Native Americans met these Europeans, they came into contact with diseases, such as smallpox and measles, that they had never experienced before. At least one half of all Native Americans, and possibly many more than that, were unable to overcome these diseases and died.

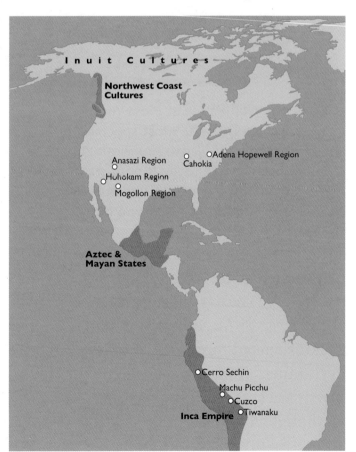

This map highlights some of the main early American cultures.

Guns were also disastrous for Native Americans. At first, only the Europeans had guns, which enabled them to overcome native peoples in fights and battles. Eventually, Native American groups obtained guns and used them in conflicts with each other. Native American groups were also forced to take sides and fight in wars between the French and British.

An Ojibwe mother and baby, photographed around 1880.

The Ojibwes traded furs with the French for guns. They used these new weapons to fight and drive away the Dakota Sioux and Fox peoples and take over their lands during the 18th century. They also fought with the French against the British, until the French were defeated and the British took control of Canada in 1760. In 1783, the boundary between the United States and Canada was established through the middle of Ojibwe territory.

Horses, too, had a big influence in Native American lifestyles, especially on the Great Plains. Some groups became horse breeders and traders. People were able to travel greater distances and began to hunt buffalo on horseback. Soon horses became central to Plains trade and social life.

At the end of the 1700s, people of European descent began to migrate over the Appalachian Mountains, looking for new land to farm and exploit. By the middle of the nineteenth century, they had reached the West Coast of North America. This expansion was disastrous for Native Americans.

RESERVATION LIFE

Many native peoples were pressured into moving onto **reservations** to the west. The biggest of these reservations later became the U.S. state of Oklahoma. Native Americans who tried to remain in their homelands were attacked and defeated. By the end of the 19th century, the Ojibwes were living on reservations that grew ever smaller as white settlers arrived.

New laws in the United States and Canada took away most of the control Native Americans had over their lives. They were expected to give up their cultures and adopt the ways and habits of white Americans. It became a crime to practice their traditional religions. Children were taken from their homes and placed in **boarding schools**, where they were forbidden to speak their native languages.

Despite this **persecution**, many Native Americans clung to their cultures through the first half of the twentieth century. The

Society of American Indians was founded in 1911, and its campaign for U.S. citizenship for Native Americans was successful in 1924. Other Native American organizations were formed to promote traditional cultures and to campaign politically for Native American rights.

Ojibwe leader Bitter Man was the chief of the Pillager Band around 1870.

THE ROAD TO SELF-GOVERNMENT

Despite these campaigns, Native Americans on reservations endured poverty and very low standards of living. Many of them moved away to work and live in cities, where they hoped life would be better. In most cases, they found life just as difficult. They not only faced **discrimination** and **prejudice** but also could not compete successfully for jobs against more established ethnic groups. In the 1950s, the United States forced up to half of all Ojibwes to move away from their reservations into cities.

In the 1970s, the American Indian Movement (AIM) organized large protests that attracted attention worldwide. They highlighted the problems of unemployment, discrimination, and poverty that Native Americans experienced in North America.

The AIM protests led to changes in policy. Some new laws protected the civil rights of Native Americans, while other laws allowed tribal governments to be formed. Today tribal governments have a wide range of powers. They operate large businesses and run their own schools and health care.

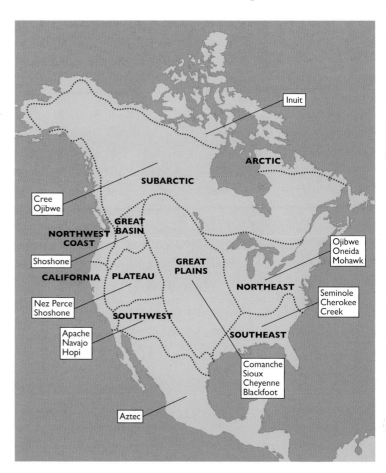

This map of North America highlights the main Native American cultural groups, along with the smaller groups, or tribes, featured in this series of books.

LAND AND ORIGINS

Chapter 1

LAND OF THE OJIBWES

One of the most numerous of the native populations in North America, the Ojibwes, also know as the Chippewas, are scattered across the United States and Canada. The Ojibwe, Potawatomi, and Ottawa tribes were originally one people. Their traditional territory stretched from the northern Great Plains near present-day Lake Winnepeg in Manitoba, Canada, to the southeastern shores of the Great Lakes in today's United States, and from central Saskatchewan to southern Ontario in today's Canada.

A young Ojibwe man wearing traditional dress at a powwow at Lake Leech in Minnesota.

ORIGIN STORY

No one knows exactly how the Ojibwes and other Native Americans came to North America. Like most native peoples, though, Ojibwes tell a traditional story to explain their origins. Long ago, only water covered the earth. Creator's helper, called Naanabozho, and his friends were floating on a raft. Naanabozho asked his friends to dive under the

The shaded area on this map shows the traditional lands of the Ojibwe people.

water and get some earth. Many tried and failed. Then Muskrat dived down and came back with sand in his paws. Naanabozho blew on the sand, spreading it over the water to create dry land. Muskrat kept diving for sand, and Naanabozho kept blowing on it until the land was large enough to support people.

MANY NAMES, ONE PEOPLE

The Ojibwes call themselves Anishinaabe (ah-nish-na-bay) or its plural, Anishinaabeg, which means "the people." They prefer to be called Anishinaabe rather than Ojibwe or Chippewa. Early French settlers called them Saulteurs. Today there are still Saulteaux, or Plains Ojibwe, in Manitoba and Saskatchewan in Canada.

Examples of traditional Ojibwe moccasins. Some nonnative historians have suggested that the words *Chippewa* and *Ojibwe* (also spelled *Ojibway* and *Ojibwa*) are translations for the term "puckered up" that describes the style of the Ojibwe moccasin.

Speaking Ojibwe

Ojibwe	Pronunciation	English
aneen	ah neen	hello
e yah'	ee yah	yes
gaween	gah ween	no
abinojeyag	a bin new je yag	children
mii gwetch	me gwetch	thank you
ogema	o ge ma	leader of an Anishinaabe band, or chief
aki	ah key	land
nibi	ne be	water

Chapter 2

HISTORY

EARLY CONTACT WITH EUROPEANS

Europeans came to North America from the late fifteenth century onward, hoping for new land, ways to acquire wealth, or religious freedom. The French began exploring the North American continent in the early 1600s looking for furs. Wanting to trade, they first came into contact with the Ojibwes (Anishinaabeg) in 1622. The traders and the Ojibwes soon built a strong **alliance** that benefited both peoples: the French got furs, while the Ojibwes received guns and other trade goods such as cast-iron pots, iron axes, and blankets. Guns helped the Ojibwes defend their territory.

Print of a French fur trader's camp. The Ojibwes were excellent hunters and trappers, and through their trade with the French, they became powerful and wealthy.

Long before contact with Europeans, an Anishinaabe **elder prophesied** "white spirits would come in numbers like sand on the lake shore, and would sweep the red race from the hunting grounds which the Great Spirit had given them."

Ojibwe (Anishinaabe) historian William Warren

The Ojibwes even kept out the powerful Haudenosaunees. They were native peoples being pushed from their land by invading Europeans (especially Dutch and British) settling on the East Coast. The Europeans pushed the Haudenosaunees (called Iroquois by the Europeans) into the eastern side of the Ojibwes' territory in what is now Michigan.

Many of the wilderness areas of the lakes and woods of Minnesota and Wisconsin have hardly changed since the time when the Ojibwes and Europeans first met.

In 1679, French trader Daniel du Luth persuaded Ojibwe leaders to attend a **council** with the Dakota-speaking people of the Seven Bands of the Teton. Du Luth helped these two traditional enemies form an alliance. Peace brought stability to the region and allowed for more trading with the French. The Ojibwes gained more hunting grounds to the west in Dakota-held territory in today's northern Minnesota and Wisconsin, while the Dakotas received a steadier supply of trade goods from the French.

Print of Ojibwe women in a birch-bark canoe gathering wild rice.

A PEOPLE ON THE MOVE

As the French fur trade moved westward, so did the Ojibwes. They spread out into the Great Lakes, the Great Plains, and what is now Michigan and Wisconsin in the United States and Ontario, Canada. Although this move resulted in a series of disputes between the Ojibwes and their neighbors, the Ojibwe-Dakota alliance lasted until 1736, when the Dakotas broke with the Ojibwes and the French over trade and land issues, killing twenty-one French allies. By 1750, the Ojibwes were occupying the land held by the Dakotas.

As more whites illegally moved onto natives' land, the Ojibwes battled the Dakotas and other neighboring tribes over rights to the remaining hunting land from the mid-1700s to the mid-1800s. Fights such as the Battle of the Brulé in 1842 eventually resulted in Ojibwes permanently driving the Dakotas west across the Mississippi River.

THE BRITISH, FRENCH, AND AMERICANS BATTLE

The Ojibwes also joined the French in trying to push the British from Canada during the French and Indian War (1754-1763), but the British took control of Canada from the French in 1760. In the Proclamation of 1763, the British recognized the Ojibwes' right to their own territory. By 1800, however, the British had forced the Ojibwes to give up over 5,000,000 acres (over 2,000,000 hectares) in Canada.

In 1776, the British and the Americans went to war over who would control the colonies in America. The Americans, with the help of many **indigenous** nations, won the war and became the United States. The **Treaty** of Paris, signed at the end of the American Revolution (1783), established the boundaries between the United States and Canada, splitting the Ojibwes' territories between the two countries.

> Although you have conquered the French, you have not conquered us. We are not your slaves. These lakes, these woods and mountains were left us by our ancestors . . . and we will part with them to none.
>
> *Ojibwe (Anishinaabe) leader Minweweh in response to the British takeover of Canada in 1760*

Native peoples sided with either the British or the French in the French and Indian War (1754–1763). British success in this war meant the Ojibwes were soon forced to give up large areas of their territory.

Life was hard for the Ojibwes during the nineteenth century as they were forced to give up more and more land to the U.S. and Canadian governments. This family was photographed in its home on a reservation in 1900.

GOVERNMENTS FORCE REMOVAL

Through treaties, both the Americans and the British in Canada forced the Ojibwes to give up land. The U.S. and Canadian governments also wanted the Ojibwes to take up Euro-American-style farming and live in what the British called "model villages."

The 1850 Robinson Superior Treaty

Ex–fur trader William Robinson **negotiated** a treaty between the Ojibwes (Anishinaabeg) living near Lake Superior and the Canadian government. In the treaty, the Ojibwes agreed to give the government some land. In return, the Canadians agreed that each Ojibwe band could select its own reservation site and each member of the bands would receive money for the land signed over to the government. The Canadians also promised that the Ojibwes would always be allowed to hunt and fish on those lands the Ojibwes gave to the government. Like many treaties, this one was quickly broken. Ojibwes were kept from hunting and fishing on the lands given to the government. As nonnatives moved onto the reservations, they took more land from the Ojibwes, and the reservations shrank in size or disappeared.

These villages were designed to force the Ojibwes to **assimilate** — to live like Euro-Americans and give up their tribal customs. By 1900, treaties had forced Ojibwes to move onto reservations. However, neither government stopped whites from illegally settling on Ojibwe land.

RESERVATION LIFE

The Canadian and U.S. governments broke their treaties with the Ojibwes. They allowed whites to illegally settle on the reservations, cutting down the timber, mining minerals, and destroying the Ojibwes' rice fields and sugar maple trees. This made life hard for Ojibwes, who were used to living in an environment that provided plenty of food.

By the early 1900s, the Ojibwes were starving. Although part of both governments' plans included teaching Ojibwes European American farming methods, what little reservation land was left was often too poor to farm. Sometimes there was not even enough land to both live on and farm.

Conditions on the early reservations were harsh. Many people were forced to live in homes that were little more than shacks.

BOARDING SCHOOLS

Canada and the United States passed laws forcing Ojibwes to send their children to boarding schools. Between the 1880s and 1940s, children as young as four were removed from their families. At school, children were punished for speaking their language. Boys spent summers working as laborers for white farmers or factory

Boys working in the blacksmith shop of an Indian boarding school. In an attempt to destroy Native American culture, many Ojibwe children were forced to leave their homes and families and go to boarding schools set up by the U.S. and Canadian governments.

owners, while girls worked as maids. They worked long hours and received little or no money for their labor. Many were not allowed to return home until they were eighteen. The Ojibwes, however, managed to hold on to their culture.

RELOCATION TO THE CITIES

In the 1950s, the United States government moved families from reservations to large cities in what the government called the "Volunteer Relocation Program" so the government could claim more of the Ojibwes' land. The program was anything but voluntary. Many Ojibwes were actually forced to move to cities such as Minneapolis and St. Paul in Minnesota. By 1970, approximately half of the Ojibwes had been moved off reservations and into urban centers.

The American Indian Movement (AIM) arose out of the government's pressure on these "urban Indians" to fully assimilate into white culture. Three Ojibwes — Dennis Banks, Clyde Bellecourt, and George Mitchell — founded AIM in Minneapolis in 1968. AIM's goal was to help Ojibwe children

Dennis Banks, one of the founders of the American Indian Movement that demanded that the government review treaties made between the United States and Native Americans.

learn more about their own culture, language, and traditions.

The idea spread to other urban Native Americans interested in keeping their cultures alive. By 1971, AIM had become a national organization and included natives on reservations and in rural areas. Their goals grew, too. AIM wanted to protect the traditions of all indigenous peoples. One way AIM and its supporters accomplished this was to bring legal cases to court, trying to get the government to uphold indigenous treaty rights such as the tribes' right to hunt, fish, and gather wild rice on their traditional lands as guaranteed by treaties.

Adam Fortunate Eagle

In 1969, Ojibwe (Anishinaabe) Adam Fortunate Eagle was among AIM members from many indigenous nations attempting to bring worldwide attention to native peoples' treaty rights. One treaty right allowed Native Americans to move to and live on land abandoned by the federal government. Alcatraz Island off the coast of California had been a prison that the government had abandoned. AIM wanted to use that land to build a Center for Native American Studies, an indigenous museum, and a school where native children could learn the history, traditions, and language of their tribes. AIM members, including Fortunate Eagle, lived on Alcatraz Island for nineteen months before the government cut off their supply of food and water and forced them to leave. The government has never allowed the center, museum, and school to be built.

TRADITIONAL WAY OF LIFE

A historic photograph of an Ojibwe woman at a sugar bush camp, cooking down the maple sap to make syrup and sugar.

A SEASONAL LIFESTYLE

For centuries, individual Ojibwe (Anishinaabe) bands moved with the seasons. Over winter, they hunted and got furs ready for trading by scraping and **tanning** them. In spring, "sugar bush" camps reunited friends and families. Relatives gathered at the family's own section of maple forest. They tapped trees and collected sap in birch-bark containers, then boiled the sap down into syrup. Once this hardened, they put it in wooden troughs and used big wooden spoons to pound it into sugar. Each family processed 500 to 600 pounds (225 to 270 kilograms) of maple sugar annually.

Ojibwe craftspeople still make traditional birch-bark canoes as a way of keeping their culture alive. Here bark is being sewn over the canoe frame with spruce thread. Birch-bark canoes are surprisingly lightweight. A canoe intended to carry nine people can itself be carried by just one person!

In summer, villages north of Lakes Superior and Huron provided a base from which families went fishing. Women made basswood-twine nets that they fished with. After catching the fish, the women washed the nets in a sumac-leaf solution to destroy fish odor, making sure fish would not shy away from the nets next time. Men made deer-bone hooks for fishing with poles, and in winter, they used wooden, fish-shaped **decoys** to lure fish to holes cut in the ice. When the waters were clear of ice, they also spearfished at night, seeing by birch-bark torches placed at the front of their canoes.

While men fished, women grew pumpkins, sweet potatoes, corn, beans, and squash. In autumn, they harvested wild foods such as nuts, berries, and rice. This was also a time for gathering herbs the people used for medicines such as goldenseal and purple coneflower, which were used to treat colds. This seasonal life remained central to Ojibwes until into the twentieth century.

The Prophecy of the Sacred Megis Shells

Megis shells were used to **barter** for trade goods such as pottery, conch shells, copper, turquoise, and other precious stones with other native peoples. The shells strung on **wampum belts** served as written records and treaties. In Ojibwe (Anishinaabe) **oral** history, Creator told the people to follow the megis shells west from their homeland along today's Saint Lawrence River until they found a place where "food grows on water." The shells led the Ojibwes to the wild rice, growing in what is now Minnesota.

HOME LIFE

Ojibwes lived in a dome-shaped house called a *wigwasigamig*. Bending wooden poles into a frame, they covered the frame with woven mats made from birch bark and cattails. A large wigwasigamig held several families. Europeans mispronounced the Ojibwes' word for their homes, calling them wigwams.

The Ojibwes made clothing from deerskins. Men wore a **loincloth**, leggings, and moccasins, while women made and wore sleeveless dresses over soft, nettle-fiber undershirts, leggings, and moccasins. The women stripped the nettle stalks and used the dried inner fibers of the plants to make clothes, somewhat like spinning wool into yarn that is then woven into cloth. In winter, people added buckskin robes. Porcupine quills decorated clothing. Trade blankets were later made into coats, pants eventually replaced leggings, and women made their dresses and leggings out of **broadcloth**. Seed beads in complex floral patterns became more common on clothing after the beads became a trade item in the mid-seventeenth century.

This Ojibwe couple, photographed in 1900, are standing in front of their wigwasigamig home. Whites had stolen so much of the Ojibwes' land, destroying their rice fields and sugar bush camps, that Ojibwe communities became among the poorest in North America during the 1900s.

A historic picture of an Ojibwe family. The young woman is wearing traditional dress, but the photographer who took the picture probably insisted she wear the feathers and a headband even though this is not traditional for the Ojibwes.

FAMILY LIFE

Ojibwes lived in family groups called **clans**. Clans were patrilineal, which means that the children belonged to their father's clan. People could not marry within their own clan. Several clans lived together in what is called a band. Friends and relatives who married into other bands often visited each other. Bands also came together for religious ceremonies, feasts, and social dances. These events gave young people opportunities to meet. Many bands make up the Ojibwe Nation.

Family values were strong among Ojibwes. Grandparents took part in raising children. White travelers often commented on Ojibwes' great affection for their children. "Even fathers are very kind to their sons," wrote one man. He added that children were quiet and polite. Children played with cornhusk dolls and ducks made out of cattails by relatives.

As was customary in the Indian community, my grandparents also helped raise several of their grandchildren and sometimes provided a home for other extended family members. They taught their children about the northern seasons, hard work, generosity, the value of relatives, and they imparted stories and songs, all in the Ojibwe language.

Brenda Child, in Boarding School Seasons, *1995*

GOVERNMENT

Ojibwe bands acted independently of one other. Each elected its own leader, the *ogimah*, and his advisers, called *anikeh-ogimauk*. Leaders were chosen by **consensus**, meaning the people all agreed on who the leaders would be. The people selected leaders who were considerate, wise, and willing to put the needs of the people first.

This photograph, taken sometime near the end of the nineteenth century, shows the Ojibwe Chief Skinaway (left, with arms folded). The man with the drum is Chief Wadena, who, in 1902, led a protest against the government's forced removal of the Ojibwes from the Mille Lacs Band Reservation to White Earth Reservation. Both men have been photographed wearing non-Ojibwe feathered headdresses.

When the U.S. and Canadian governments began treaty negotiations, Ojibwes found that whites expected to deal with a single tribal leader. They forced the Ojibwes to change their traditional government. Bands formed what became known as the Grand Council and elected a primary ogimah. The Grand Council was responsible for declaring war, negotiating peace, and developing laws.

Sam Yankee, Ojibwe Leader

Sam Yankee's Ojibwe (Anishinaabe) name was Ayshpun, meaning "very high up." Born sometime around 1900, Ayshpun was a Midé, a religious leader in the Midewiwin, a group of healers. He also had the honor of being a drum carrier, the person chosen to care for the ceremonial drum.

The Mille Lacs Band of Ojibwe Indians in Minnesota elected him chair of the Reservation Business Committee, part of the Mille Lacs government. Its members oversee tribal affairs. Ayshpun helped develop programs that resulted in building new homes for band members and a community center where children could learn Ojibwe traditions. He also taught the language, traditional songs, and drumming, and he shared the oral history of the people with youngsters. Ayshpun led his people during a time of great change, from the 1960s until his death in 1975.

BELIEFS

Many Ojibwes believe in the Creator, who is neither male nor female. The Creator shares power with others — the trees, plants, animals, water, other spirits, and people — that are often messengers for the Creator, bringing the Midewiwin (a religious society of healers) dreams and spirit guides.

Dreams are an important part of Ojibwe religious beliefs. Boys and girls are encouraged to seek **visions**. During vision **quests**, Ojibwes receive dreams. They may also receive special lessons from an animal who becomes their spirit guide, or they may be shown how to use a medicine plant in a new way. A spirit guide comes to a person when and how the spirit guide decides.

Ojibwe women, wearing jingle dresses, perform dances at their powwow at the Leech Lake Reservation in Minnesota. The jingle dress is sacred to the Ojibwes and originates from an old story about an elder who received a vision telling him to make a dress that jingled for his sick daughter.

TRADITIONAL HEALERS

Depending on local traditions, there are four or eight levels of membership in the Midewiwin. Members are called Midé. They advance by completing lessons in proper behavior and in identifying and using medicines. They also learn how to read Midewiwin records written on birch-bark scrolls. Those at the highest levels know how to use rare herbs.

"Ojibwe Tea"

The Midewiwin believe that living a patient, moderate, truthful, and respectful life, combined with using medicine plants given by the Creator, prolongs life. In the 1930s, a white nurse named Renee Caisse treated very sick patients with a blend of herbs the Midewiwin use. She called this blend "Ojibwe tea." The recovery rate was impressive. Scientific studies show "Ojibwe tea" reduces pain and increases the number of cells that fight diseases. The herbs in "Ojibwe tea" are some of the 637 herbs used by indigenous peoples that have been accepted for use by the United States government.

The society used to hold ceremonies in a special lodge that was not covered unless the weather was bad. This way nonmembers could view them. However, the Midé conducted ceremonies in a special language with special songs that only members understood.

Among Ojibwes, native healers have traditionally been given the same respect as modern-day doctors because they can use herbs to treat sickness in people and bring them back to health. To become an Ojibwe healer takes a lifetime of education and practice.

Midewiwin healer Maymasushkowaush, known to whites as Axel Pasey, poses with his wife and daughter in this 1936 photo. Although he wears traditional clothing, the feathers and headbands are not traditional Ojibwe. Many whites believed all Indians wore feathers.

Ojibwe Legends

Ojibwe elder Lee Staples remembers the stories he was told by his mother when he was a child. "I could hardly wait until the first snow fell because that meant the telling of legends could start. We were told that if the legends were told in the summer – out of season – we'd end up with a frog in our bed."

Staples's mother believed the stories were significant: "Listening to the legends, you could acquire some power or gift from the spirits she was talking about. So she would get upset with me if I fell asleep."

The Ojibwes' most important hero is Naanabozho (also known as Wenabozho or Manabozho). Several stories tell how he helped the animals. For example, the Ojibwes say that he gave the tortoise a shell, so that it would not be eaten by the otter. A similar story tells how Naanabozho covered the porcupine's back with clay and stuck thorns in it to protect it from bear attacks.

The story of the tortoise shell features the North American river otter. It can eat shellfish but not tortoises.

Today, although metal buckets are used instead of birch-bark containers to collect the sap of maple trees, people still have to work hard to enjoy maple syrup.

Naanabozho was sent to Earth by the Creator to teach the Ojibwe how to live properly. The following story is a lesson to young Ojibwes about how people should work hard to find their food.

When the world was young, the maple trees were running with thick syrup. The people became very lazy, lying around under the maple trees and letting the syrup run into their mouths from broken twigs. They had no need to fish or hunt or look after their crops.

Naanabozho did not want the people to become fat and lazy, so he climbed to the tops of the trees and poured water into them. Since that time, maple trees have only produced a watery liquid. The Ojibwes had to learn to make cuts in the wood, craft birch-bark containers, collect lots of the liquid, then boil off the water to obtain maple syrup. And Naanabozho also made sure that no liquid ran out of the trees at the times of year when the Ojibwes should be hunting, fishing, and farming.

Chapter 4

OJIBWE LIFE TODAY

OJIBWE GOVERNMENTS

Today, about 120,000 Ojibwes (Anishinaabeg) live in Michigan, Wisconsin, Minnesota, and North Dakota in the United States and about 75,000 in Ontario, Manitoba, and Saskatchewan in Canada. They are the fourth-largest Native American group in the United States and the third-largest in Canada.

Each Ojibwe reservation in Canada elects its own ogimah and council. The reservations (called reserves in Canada) also send representatives to the Union of Ontario Indians (UOI). UOI works with the Canadian government, trying to insure that the indigenous peoples receive the health and educational programs to which they are entitled.

The red areas on this map mark where most of the Ojibwe reservations are today. They are widely spread over northeastern North America.

This welcome board to the Wikwemikong reserve on Manitoulin Island in Canada proudly displays photos of some of its well-known residents, many of them celebrated artists.

In the United States, individual Ojibwe bands elect tribal councils consisting of a board with a chairperson. The Mille Lacs Band in Minnesota, however, has a governmental system similar to that of the United States.

CONTEMPORARY LIFE

Ojibwe families who live on reservations today remain very close. Parents, children, grandparents, and other relatives get together often. They continue the tradition of hospitality and concern for their relatives and community. Ojibwes try to help each other and work for their communities to keep them strong.

On or off the reservation, Ojibwes live in the same types of houses as nonnatives. Ojibwes own TVs, radios, computers, video games, stoves, refrigerators, cars, and telephones. Like the rest of the world, bands are linked by high-speed Internet connections.

Traditional drumming plays a part in the weekly high school powwow on the Lac Courte Oreilles reservation in Wisconsin.

I may be an Urban Indian, but . . . the reserve is still deep within me. . . . As my mother says, I know home will always be there. So will the mosquitoes and the gossip and the relatives who still treat you like you are twelve years old . . . and those who walk in my moccasins know the rest.

Drew Hayden Taylor in Funny, You Don't look Like One: Observations from a Blue-Eyed Ojibway, *1998*

Children play ball in the yard, go to school, and do homework. Many speak three languages — English, French, and Ojibwe. Some take part in traditional ceremonies and have learned how to build birch-bark canoes, weave baskets, or bead clothing. They also help their relatives harvest wild rice and make maple sugar.

HEALTH ISSUES

Many Ojibwes suffer from an illness called diabetes, which is often caused by eating unhealthy foods. Most bands tackle this problem by making people aware of what causes diabetes and encouraging them to eat more healthily.

Another widespread health problem is **addiction** to alcohol or drugs. The tribes are trying various ways to cure these addictions.

WORKING OUTDOORS

The Ojibwe bands use the natural **resources** around them to provide employment. For example, in Wisconsin, the Red Cliff Band, the Bad River La Pointe Band, the Lac Courte Oreilles Band, and the Lac du Flambeau Band of Lake Superior Chippewa each own their own tribal hatchery to stock local rivers, lakes, and streams with fish. The Lac Courte Oreilles Band also owns a cranberry marsh at Chief Lake, a **hydroelectric** facility, and a lumber mill.

WILD RICE PRODUCTION

Traditionally the Ojibwes harvested wild rice around the edges of lakes, and they still cultivate the old rice beds. The Leech Lake Band harvests rice from forty lakes in Minnesota. The Bad River La Pointe Band gathers rice from marshes at the edge of Lake Superior and holds a wild rice festival every August. Since 2004, young Ojibwes have taken part in a project to plant wild rice along lake shores in Michigan, where there was no wild rice left.

Today, Ojibwes still harvest *manomin*, wild rice, in the traditional way. One person uses long poles to push the canoes through the fields, while another uses cedar sticks to bend the stalks and knock the grain into the canoe.

Slot machines at Mille Lacs Reservation Grand Casino in Minnesota. Money generated by casino gambling has enabled the Ojibwes to start their own schools where children can learn about traditional culture and language.

LEISURE BUSINESSES

Tribal **casinos** have been built on many Ojibwe reservations in Wisconsin, Minnesota, and Michigan. They have provided Ojibwes with jobs and money for other enterprises such as a horse-breeding business, craft shops, and construction companies, as well as funds for policing, schools, and medical clinics. Other leisure facilities also bring money to the tribes. For example, the Mille Lacs Band in Minnesota owns a golf course, a lakeside fishing resort, and a cinema, as well as two casinos.

The Great Spirit Circle Trail

Manitoulin Island in Lake Huron is the largest freshwater island in the world. It contains historic Native American sites that are known to be around ten thousand years old.

Today the island is home to several Ojibwe groups, who joined together in 1998 to create and run a tourist business, the Great Spirit Circle Trail. Tourists are offered insights into traditional Ojibwe life. They can choose from a wide range of activities, including riding trails, canoe and walking tours, craft and food workshops, and camping Ojibwe-style.

Nay Ah Shing Schools

Tribal colleges in the United States and Canada celebrate cultural understanding by promoting the language, culture, and history of the Ojibwes. In 1999, the Mille Lacs Band opened the Nay Ah Shing primary and secondary schools. The schools are a major step forward in the Ojibwes' efforts to recover their cultural **heritage**. Twelve teachers instruct 270 students in the Ojibwe language. Students learn the language and history and participate in traditional activities such as gathering rice, making maple sugar, hunting, fishing, and drumming.

Here an Ojibwe student at a Nay Ah Shing school uses a computer to learn about his special cultural heritage.

SPORTING SUCCESS

Ojibwes have also made their mark in sports, especially in pro hockey. Ted Nolan was National Hockey League (NHL) Coach of the Year in 1997. He credits his achievements to the cultural traditions his parents taught him — traditions like working together, respecting elders, and making decisions as a group.

Hockey coach Ted Nolan has set up a charity, the Ted Nolan Foundation, to promote healthy lifestyles for young Native American people.

A cultural tile mural created at the Mille Lacs Band's Nay Ah Shing school.

> Nothing gives me more pleasure than to speak the language of my ancestors. I'm trying to keep my native Ojibwe tongue alive so that my **descendants** will be able to feel that same joy. Each morning I try to say a prayer in Ojibwe. I like to honor my past by always introducing myself in my native tongue.
>
> *Dr. Arne Vainio, Mille Lacs Band*

LITERATURE AND ART

Artist Rebecca Belmore uses humor in her visual and performance art to help nonnatives see the often silly ways in which native people are depicted in popular culture. Her shows at the Canadian Museum of Civilization in Hull, Quebec, include "(I'm a) High-Tech Teepee Trauma Mama."

Sculptor Ron Noganosh also uses humor to get the meaning of his art across to people. "If they stop and laugh I got their attention, and then maybe they'll take the time to look around at it a little bit more and see what's going on," he explains. Many of his works were created from items people have thrown away. In his sculpture *Will the Turtle Be Unbroken?* Planet Earth, dying from pollution, sits on a turtle shell that is carried through space on the starship *Enterprise*.

Louise Erdrich, the granddaughter of a tribal chief, has written both adult novels and children's books. In many of them, she describes about how the loss of land, children, and cultural traditions to whites' assimilation policies affect Ojibwe families. Her characters rely on humor and strong ties to traditions to get them through often harsh lives. *The Birchbark House, The Game of Silence,* and *The Porcupine Year* are a set of children's books Erdrich wrote about the lives of an Ojibwe girl and her family and tribe in the middle of the nineteenth century.

Ojibwe Comic Books

The Mille Lacs Band in Minnesota developed its first educational comic book in 1996 as an "opportunity to share our heritage and culture with others," explained Melanie Benjamin, former chief executive of the Mille Lacs Band. Their second comic book was released in 1999.

In *A Hero's Voice,* Georgie and Jennie learn about true heroic Ojibwe (Anishinaabe) leaders by listening to their grandfather's stories. In *Dreams of Looking Up,* Mary and her family discover the importance of their people's traditions, customs, and culture.

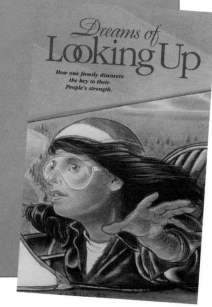

CURRENT OJIBWE ISSUES

Chapter 5

TREATY RIGHTS

In the 1980s, Ojibwes began taking the U.S. and Canadian governments to court over broken treaties. The Ojibwes proved in court that they had the right, as stated in the 1837 and 1850 treaties, to hunt and fish on the lands turned over to the U.S. and Canadian governments. The court agreed and said the Ojibwes could hunt and fish on what had been their lands at the time these treaties were signed.

This angered many nonnatives, who now claimed ownership of the land and who fished the waters. They claimed that the Ojibwes were threatening the supply of fish, but this was proven in court to be incorrect. Instead, it was **pollutants** from nonnative industries and nonnative sports anglers who had reduced fish populations.

The legal battles went all the way to the U.S. Supreme Court, which upheld the Ojibwes' rights to hunt and fish beyond the boundaries of the reservations. Today, white resort owners and sports anglers continue to **harass** Ojibwe fishermen despite court rulings.

A press conference at the Mille Lacs Band reservation in Minnesota announcing the 1999 Supreme Court ruling upholding the treaty of 1837. This treaty allowed the Ojibwes to hunt and fish on land that had once belonged to them.

White Earth Land Recovery Project

The White Earth Land Recovery Project (WELRP) was formed by Winona LaDuke in 1989 to push for the recovery of lands that were taken from the White Earth Indian Reservation in northeastern Minnesota more than one hundred years ago. The project also seeks to preserve traditional Ojibwe farming methods. It produces and sells traditional foods through the "Native Harvest" label and also collects and preserves old varieties of crop seeds, which it gives them to anyone who wishes to plant them.

Curing Addictions

A residential three-month program for drug and alcohol users at the Oshki Manidoo Center in Bemidji, Minnesota, was set up in 2008 by the White Earth Reservation tribal council. It detaches young people from their addictions and provides a range of **therapies**. At the same time, it offers opportunities to explore and follow traditional Ojibwe culture and values as an alternative lifestyle and way of thinking.

Through this and many other projects, such as WELRP, the modern Ojibwes are successfully preserving their traditional lifestyles, language, and culture.

Members of the Saginaw Chippewa Indian Tribe of Michigan celebrate the opening of the National Museum of the American Indian in Washington, DC.

TIMELINE

1622	First contact between Ojibwes (Anishinaabeg) and Europeans (French traders) leads to an trade alliance.
1679	Daniel du Luth negotiates a peace agreement between the Ojibwes and the Dakotas in which the Ojibwes gain more hunting grounds in northern Minnesota and Wisconsin.
1736	War breaks out between the Ojibwes and Dakotas over French trade.
1745–50	Ojibwes settle in the region of Lake Mille Lacs in modern Minnesota.
1754–1763	Ojibwes join the French against the British in the French and Indian War.
1760	British take control of Canada from the French.
1763	British recognize the Ojibwes' right to their own territory.
1783	Treaty of Paris splits the Ojibwes' territory between Canada and the United States.
1825	Treaty council held at Prairie du Chien, Wisconsin, establishes the boundaries between the Ojibwes and Dakotas.
1837	Treaty of 1837 protects hunting, fishing, and gathering rights on Ojibwe land taken by the U.S. government.
1842	Battle of the Brulé results in Ojibwes driving the Dakotas west across the Mississippi River.
1850	Canadian government and Ojibwes sign Robinson Superior Treaty.
1855	Mille Lacs Band signs a treaty that creates a 61,000-acre (24,700 ha) reservation at Lake Mille Lacs; the U.S. government also negotiates with other bands, promising to create reservations around eastern Michigan, which it never does.

1862	Dakota War begins; Mille Lacs Band warriors end up defending nonnatives.
1880s	U.S. government passes assimilation policies.
1891	U.S. Congress declares all native children must attend boarding schools.
1902	U.S. government officials sell land on the Mille Lacs Reservation and force members of that band to move to White Earth Reservation.
1934	Congress passes the Indian Reorganization Act, recognizing indigenous people's right to self-government.
1942	Canadian government illegally seizes the majority of the Stony Point Reserve, forcibly relocating the band to the nearby Kettle Point Reserve.
1950s–1960s	Many Ojibwes are forced to move off their reservations to large cities such as Minneapolis and St. Paul, Minnesota.
1968	Three Ojibwes found the American Indian Movement in Minneapolis, Minnesota.
1974–77	Ojibwes of Sabaskong Bay in Ontario defy the Canadian government and begin running their own schools.
1984–94	Five reservations are established in Michigan.
1989	Winona LaDuke forms the White Earth Land Recovery Project to recover Ojibwe lands in Minnesota.
1999	U.S. Supreme Court upholds the Treaty of 1837, stating that Ojibwes have a treaty right to hunt, fish, and gather on lands taken away from them by the government; Ojibwes continue to be harassed when trying to hunt or fish as guaranteed by treaty.
2004	Youth project to replant wild rice along lake shores in Michigan begins.
2008	Oshki Manidoo Center set up in Bemidji, Minnesota, to combat drug and alcohol addiction.

GLOSSARY

addiction: the state of being unable to resist consuming certain substances, such as alcohol or drugs.

alliance: an agreement between two groups to work together on a common goal.

ancestor: a person from whom an individual or group is descended.

assimilate: to bring into conformity with the customs and attitudes of a group or nation.

barter: to exchange goods rather than pay money for them.

boarding schools: places where students must live at the school.

broadcloth: a thick cloth woven from wool.

casinos: buildings that have slot machines, card games, and other gambling games.

clan: a group of related families.

consensus: an agreement among all individuals in a group to an opinion or position.

council: a group of people who meet regularly to discuss issues or manage something.

culture: the arts, beliefs, and customs that make up a people's way of life.

decoy: something used to attract animals into a trap.

descendants: all the children and children's children of an individual or group; those who come after.

discrimination: unjust treatment usually because of a person's race or sex.

elder: an older person.

environment: objects and conditions all around that affect living things and communities.

floodplain: the area of land beside a river or stream that is covered with water during a flood.

harass: to put aggressive pressure on a person or persons.

heritage: cultural traditions that are passed down from grandparents and parents to children for many years.

hydroelectric: having to do with the use of flowing water to generate electricity.

ice age: a period of time when the earth is very cold and lots of water in the oceans turns to ice.

indigenous: originating in a particular country or region.

irrigation: any system for watering the land to grow plants.

loincloth: a piece of cloth wrapped around the hips.

migration: movement from one place to another.

negotiate: to discuss with others to come to an agreement.

oral: spoken rather than written.

persecution: treating someone or a certain group of people badly over a period of time.

pollutants: substances that make air, water, or land dirty or impure.

prejudice: dislike or injustice that is not based on reason or experience.

prophesy: to tell of something that one feels will happen in the future.

quest: an adventurous journey to seek something.

reservation: land set aside by the U.S. government for specific Native American tribes to live on.

resources: materials available for use.

tan: to make into leather by soaking an animal skin in a special solution.

therapies: treatments to heal or relieve a disorder.

treaties: agreements between several nations.

visions: things that are not from this world but the supernatural one; visions resemble dreams, but the person is awake.

wampum belts: different-colored beads made from shells strung into belts in unique designs, which serve as reminders of historical events, laws, and treaties.

MORE RESOURCES

WEBSITES:

http://www.bigorrin.org/chippewa_kids.htm
Online Ojibwe Indian Fact Sheet for Kids in question-and-answer form with useful links.

http://www.kstrom.net/isk/food/wildrice.html
This website tells the story of Ojibwe wild rice gathering.

http://www.kstrom.net/isk/food/maple.html
This website tells the story of Ojibwe sugar bush camps.

http://www.millelacsband.com/Page_MoccasinTelegraph.aspx
The Mille Lacs Band of Ojibwe members write about their traditional culture and what it is to be a Native American today.

http://www.millelacsband.com/pdf/Visitors%20GuideLR.pdf
The Mille Lacs Band of Ojibwe Visitors' Guide.

http://www.mpm.edu/wirp/
The Indian Country Wisconsin website contains pages about Ojibwe culture, history, oral traditions, and treaties.

http://www.native-languages.org/chippewa.htm
This website contains numerous links to pages about the Ojibwe language, culture, and history, and to Ojibwe band websites.

http://www.ojibwe.org/
Site for the award-winning PBS documentary series about the history and culture of the Ojibwe people in the United States.

http://www.ojibwe-language.com/
A website to help people learn the Ojibwe language.

http://www.wisconsinstories.org/archives/ojibwehistory/index.cfm?action=ojibwehistory
Video clips from Wisconsin Public Television in which Ojibwe Eddie Benton-Benai talks about the culture and history of his people.

DVD:

Jim Northrup: With Reservations. The Center for International Education, 2011.

Books:

Benton-Benai, Edward. *The Mishomis Book: The Voice of the Ojibway.* University of Minnesota Press, 2010.

Ditchfield, Christin. *The Chippewa (True Books: American Indians).* Children's Press, 2006.

Erdrich, Louise. *The Birchbark House.* Hyperion, 2002.

Erdrich, Louise. *The Game of Silence.* HarperCollins, 2005.

Erdrich, Louise. *The Porcupine Year.* HarperCollins, 2010.

Kallen, Stuart. *Native Americans of the Great Lakes (North American Indians).* Kidhaven, 2003.

King, David C. *First People.* DK Children, 2008.

King, David C. *Ojibwe (First Americans).* Benchmark Books, 2006.

Levine, Michelle. *The Ojibwe (Native American Histories).* Lerner Classroom, 2007.

Lomberg, Michelle. *Ojibwa (Aboriginal Peoples of Canada).* Weigl Educational, 2009.

Murdoch, David S. *North American Indian (DK Eyewitness Books).* DK Children, 2005.

Peacock, Thomas. *The Four Hills of Life.* Minnesota Historical Society Press, 2011.

Peacock, Thomas. *The Good Path: Ojibway Learning and Activity Book for Kids.* Minnesota Historical Society Press, 2009.

Smithyman, Kathryn, and Bobby Kalman. *Nations of the Western Great Lakes (Native Nations of North America).* Crabtree Publishing Company, 2002.

Walker, Niki. *Life in an Anishinabe Camp (Native Nations of North America).* Crabtree Publishing Company, 2002.

THINGS TO THINK ABOUT AND DO

A Variety of Homes

The Ojibwes' neighbors to the West were the Dakotas and to the East were the Haudenosaunees. Each of these native peoples lived in very different types of houses. Research these houses on the web or in books. Draw a Dakota teepee, an Ojibwe wigwasigamig, and a Haudenosaunee longhouse. Write about how each of these homes is different from the others.

Country Life, City Life

Many Ojibwes were forced to move to cities during the 1950s. How would life be different for these people who had grown up gathering wild rice, making maple sugar, growing vegetables, hunting game, and fishing? Write an essay on what you think.

Ojibwe Beading

Look at the designs on pages 10 and 11 of this book. Using beads, paste, and a piece of cloth, create a floral design similar to the ones Ojibwes sewed on their clothing.

Creative Recycling

Ojibwe Artist Ron Noganosh uses odds and ends that people usually throw away to create his artwork. Collect some items from home and see what sort of artwork you can create.

INDEX